This Grateful Heart

This Grateful Heart

Psalms and Prayers for a New Day

ALDEN SOLOVY

CENTRAL CONFERENCE OF AMERICAN RABBIS

In memory of my father, Jack P. Solovy, z"l
—Alden Solovy

Library of Congress Cataloging-in-Publication Data

Names: Solovy, Alden T., 1957– author.
Title: This grateful heart : psalms and prayers for a new day / Alden Solovy.
Description: New York : CCAR Press, Reform Judaism Publishing, [2017] |
    Includes bibliographical references and index.
Identifiers: LCCN 2016056401 (print) | LCCN 2016059258 (ebook) | ISBN
    9780881232882 (pbk. : alk. paper) | ISBN 9780881232950
Subjects: LCSH: Prayer--Judaism. | Jewish religious poetry, American. |
    Jewish meditations. | Spiritual life--Judaism.
Classification: LCC BM665 .S55 2017 (print) | LCC BM665 (ebook) | DDC
    296.4/5--dc23
LC record available at https://lccn.loc.gov/2016056401

ISBN: 978-0-88123-288-2

Book interior designed and composed by Scott-Martin Kosofsky
at The Philidor Company, Rhinebeck, New York.

CCAR Press, 355 Lexington Avenue, New York, NY 10017
(212) 972-3636
www.ccarpress.org
Printed in U.S.A.
10 9 8 7 6 5 4 3 2 1

Contents

Foreword

by Rabbi Menachem Creditor

> *Do not make your prayer static; rather pour out suppli-*
> *cation and mercy before the Omnipresent.*
> —RABBI SHIMON, *Pirkei Avot* 2:18

> *Dear Lord, grant me the grace of wonder. Surprise me,*
> *amaze me, awe me in every crevice of Your universe.*
> —RABBI ABRAHAM JOSHUA HESCHEL

PRAYER can be so many things: quiet acknowledgment, public response, individual protest, rapturous surrender. So very many things. And this is as it should be, for the expressions and experiences of prayer are as manifold as the human heart, itself a refraction of God's own. After all, as the Rabbis teach, "God desires the prayers of the heart" (Babylonian Talmud, *Sanhedrin* 106b).

A prayerful soul, aware of and yearning for the possibility of sacred encounter, is not inured to the world-as-it-is, does not experience drudgery while re-walking worn paths, cannot remain calm upon gazing at the sky. For the afflictions of dissociation and boredom, prayer is the antidote.

When does one learn how to pray?

When "the world is too much with us" (William Wordsworth), when "evening falls so hard" (Paul Simon), when experience makes us "scared of the life that's inside" (Sara Bareilles), you know. When you find yourself on your knees, soundly humbled by life's unexpected twists, you know. When your soul is touched by another, when the feeling of abundance explodes in your life, when your wounded heart starts pounding with healing, you know. When you rage at what's wrong, shake your fist at heaven in demand of justice in God's universe, you know.

We weep prayer. We sing prayer. We dance prayer. We march prayer. Often, the body is already praying before the mind has decided to.

The infinite expressions of human emotion and experience elude simple translation and only sometimes manage to eventually find form in words. Rarer still is the gift of an attuned liturgy, language generated by a person sensitive enough to feel as if their words are being written from within another's experience. Alden Solovy is not only an elegant writer and eloquent poet; he is an authentic inheritor of Judaism's rich historical legacy of intuitive prayer.

What kind of soul can generate these shareable prayer sparks? A soul that knows that life is, as Solovy writes, "profound in joy / profound in sorrow . . . rich in laughter / rich with tears." Life is all this and more, profound and rich, amazing and wondrous.

This beautiful volume of contemporary prayers includes all of these responses and more, spanning the rhythm of a day, the Jewish holiday cycle, sacred days of the secular calendar, and life moments both joyous and dark. In other words, these prayers are for and of the real world, offering a glimpse of the world-to-come while cherishing this one.

A text from the Talmud comes to mind, upon reading (through tears, often) Solovy's prayers:

> It was taught: Rabbi Ishmael ben Elisha said: "I once entered into the Holy of Holies and saw God, seated upon a high and exalted throne. God said to me: 'Ishmael, My child, bless Me!' I replied: 'May it be Your will that Your mercy conquer Your anger, that Your mercy wash over Your stricter qualities, so that You

might behave with Your children mercifully and see beyond the letter of the law.' And God nodded to me. Here we learn that the blessing of an ordinary person must not be considered lightly in your eyes." (Babylonian Talmud, *B'rachot* 7a, adapted)

In Jewish tradition, God seeks blessing from ordinary people. Like you and me. And especially, like Alden Solovy.

When someone is able to enter God's holy space with unadorned grace, has the strength to bring others along that well-worn, sparkling sacred path, and helps open our eyes so that we might see beyond letters and words to truly touch and be touched by God, we should not take that lightly. We should, instead, celebrate our newfound (recovered, actually) ability to be surprised by the world once again, to feel the gift of awe, to pour our deepest gratitude into every crevice of the universe.

The prayers in this magic collection are channels to the Divine, opportunities for communion, ringing reminders that Jewish spirituality is so very, very alive.

For this, I offer the thanks of my own grateful heart.

Introduction

ONCE, I fell in love with a prayer. The way you might fall in love with a poem by Mary Oliver or a song by Leonard Cohen. The way that makes you want to sing it again and again. I've fallen in love with classic prayers from all over our siddur: *Mah Tovu, Y'did Nefesh, Shomei-a T'filah*. I've fallen in love with the prayers and music of the poets, liturgists, and musicians of our day. My love affair with the siddur and with Jewish prayer has been going on for nearly fifty years.

Like any love affair, it's had rocky moments. Compromises were made. There are prayers that don't resonate for me. I change words. I change the meaning in my mind. I skip some altogether. When I watched Ami, *z"l*, my wife of twenty-seven years, die of traumatic brain injury, when I watched my daughter's struggle in the aftermath, prayer seemed to lose that robust and nourishing sense of meaning that I relied upon.

And yet prayer has not let me down. Even in those empty moments, prayer has found its way back into my heart. Sometimes through the siddur, which is a vast resource of history, emotion, and teaching. Sometimes through my own writing.

Prayer reminds me of simple truths. We are surrounded by holiness. By beauty. By wonder and awe. At the same time, we must live life as it is offered to us, sometimes messy, sometimes challenging, potentially painful, potentially traumatic, a mixed bag of joys and sorrows. No matter what, our lives are enriched by prayer. Prayer gives our hearts a voice.

There's no moment too small for a prayer. Or too large for that matter. A single petal of a rose. A field of wildflowers. A birth. A death. And there's no moment too small or too large for gratitude.

Composing prayers is a natural expression of my desire to move closer to God. In response to various life tragedies I began a spiritual journey of prayer, meditation, daily journaling, and making gratitude lists. This writing evolved into a regular practice of composing prayers.

The act of creating a prayer is healing. One aspect of healing comes in recognizing the yearning, the deep desire that needs a voice. Another element of that healing is the writing itself, which attaches those yearnings to language—often lyrical, but sometimes blunt—evoking a prayer of the heart. I recommend it.

In our siddur, whether it's *Mishkan T'filah* or any other Jewish prayer book, we say that God is *shomei-a t'filah*, the One who hears our prayers. The faith that our prayers are heard gives prayer power. We don't have to be alone in grief. We have a witness, perhaps the ultimate Witness, to both our troubles and our triumphs. Our extraordinary times will be heard by the One who hears.

The core of *This Grateful Heart* is bringing a modern voice of prayer into the routine flow of our lives. Waking in the morning. Going to sleep at night. The change of seasons. Holy days. Regular days. Shabbat. We recognize that the regular practice of gratitude in prayer will enrich our days and help us get through the tougher times.

To create this collection, I reread every one of my pieces, more than six hundred liturgical works. As you might imagine, with such a large body of work I'd lost my connection with some of these prayers. Creating *This Grateful Heart* gave me an opportunity to reconnect with my own prayers, to remember the love that went into the creation of each piece. To remember why I wrote each one. That was a real gift.

This book contains pieces meant to be used for both personal and communal prayer. That was a key challenge in creating this anthology. By design, most of the works in *This Grateful Heart* can do "double-duty." While individuals and families will find voice for their hopes and aspirations, rabbis and cantors will also find prayers and readings that engage us in *t'filah*—in worship— as well as a rich resource for counseling congregants.

The flow and organization of the prayers, matching the rhythms of our lives, gives *This Grateful Heart* a unique warmth and charm. The experience is much different than reading a classic anthology organized by topic. *This Grateful Heart* connects deeply into the flow of time and seasons. It can be used in private prayer and in communal worship. As a book of prayers, it's versatile. As a spiritual guide, it brings both intimacy and tenderness, as well as a sense of strength.

We pray in joy, fear, sorrow, and loss. We pray to celebrate, to mourn, to create a connection with beauty, hope, and love. Prayer is an expression of our inner voice. We pray as an expression of gratitude. I hope that people will see *This Grateful Heart* as a prayer book, a resource kit, a spiritual practice, an inspiration, and a source of hope.

Prayer and gratitude elevate us. Prayer and gratitude light our way. This is not always easy. My own love affair with prayer has had rocky moments, moments when I resisted prayer, moments when I resisted my higher gut instinct that prayer would guide me to healing. That's one of the reasons that this book moves with the cycles of our lives. Any day a prayer is needed, any day someone decides to say a prayer or to deepen a personal prayer practice, this book can be a doorway.

Most of all, I hope that this book will help you fall in love with prayer. Or rediscover a love of prayer. Or spark a deepening of that love. Let *This Grateful Heart* become part of your own grateful heart. May the words of your heart lift you, shine within you, and bring you joy, comfort, and peace.

AUTHOR'S NOTE

Personalizing the Prayers. Some prayers in this volume are written to be personalized in a variety of ways, such as modifying the gender references and inserting names of individuals who are sick or in need of a blessing. The main symbols are brackets, slashes and blank lines. Here's a guide to the symbols that indicate choices for customizing the prayers.

Brackets [ ] Brackets are used to either provide instructions for the person saying the prayer or to identify optional lines. They are also used identify lists in which only one choice is needed. The choices in these lists are separated by slashes.

Slashes / Slashes typically denote a gender choice, such as him/her, or a choice to say the prayer in the first-person singular or the first-person plural, such as I/we.

Blank lines _____ Blank lines are most commonly used to indicate the opportunity to insert an individual's name, typically in a healing prayer or a *Yizkor* prayer. A blank line can also indicate the opportunity to customize the prayer to an event.

Hebrew words in the text of the prayers are in italics, except when that word has entered the English dictionary, such as Torah.

Acknowledgments

God of creativity,
Heavenly hand of beauty and wonder,
Bless those who have supported me,
Helped and encouraged me,
Sharing their wisdom and talents
As I pursue the call to write In service to Your Holy Name.
You have sent men and women,
Teachers and counselors,
Friends and guides,
To travel with me on this journey of prayer and blessing.
May their enthusiasm return to them, tenfold, as gifts.
May their wisdom continue to echo into the world
And into the lives of those around them,
Yielding holiness and love in the light of their presence.
Bless them, sustain them and grant them
Health and happiness,
Joy and peace.
Amen.

THIS HAS BEEN quite a journey for this grateful heart of mine. Who could imagine when I first began posting prayers online six years ago, that a community of people who love and yearn for prayer would find a voice in this work. Thanks to all of you who've supported me by reading my prayers and poetry online. Thanks for your comments and your care. Seeing my readership grow is a source of great joy and inspiration. Your encouragement has sustained me.

One of the many blessings has been the number of individuals—clergy and others—who've offered insights and advice on my work. I've turned to many of you when challenged by a particular topic. Others have reached out to me, suggesting topics for new prayers. Still others have inspired my work with their own teaching and writing. The list is long and lovely. Here, I'm focusing on the people who had an impact on the content of this volume, whether they know it or not: Rabbi Ruth Abusch-Magder, Rabbi Bob Carroll, Rabbi Stephanie Clark Covitz, Anita Diamant, Rabbi Sharyn Henry, Cantor Evan Kent, Rabbi Paul Kipnes, Rabbi Zoe Klein, Rabbi Andrea London, Rabbi Joseph Meszler, Josh Nelson, Galeet Dardashti, and Rhonda Rosenheck. My apologies to anyone whom I might of missed.

I'm also touched by the people who read the manuscript and provided heartfelt words of support. Remarkably kind and loving endorsements came from Rabba Yaffa Epstein, Rabbi Karyn Kedar, and Rabbi Peter Knobel.

Rabbi Menachem Creditor's introduction is stunning and beautiful, both in its teaching about prayer and in its generosity in praise for this book. Brother, teacher, friend: I'm both thrilled and humbled that your are part of this project.

A word of deep thanks to those who had a direct hand in creating *This Grateful Heart*. First, thanks to the CCAR Publishing Council for supporting this project. The team at CCAR Press is a joy. Thank you, Deborah Smilow, Rabbi Dan Medwin, and Carly Linden from the CCAR staff, and to Debra Corman for copy-editing, to Michelle Kwitkin-Close for proofreading, and to Scott-Martin Kosofsky for design and compositing. Thanks to Sasha Smith for keen comments on the manuscript and for your sensitivity to language. Thanks to Ortal Bensky for your many creative ideas and great energy for marketing this book. Thanks to Rabbi Steven Fox, CCAR Chief Executive, for supporting this book. A special thanks to Rabbi Donald Goor who chaired the book review committee and then became part of the editing team, exploring and challenging the meaning and intent of each prayer. My deepest thanks to Rabbi Hara Person, who conceived this project. You've been coach, consultant, editor, advocate and friend, while simultaneously managing the business aspects of this project. There would be no book without you. *This Grateful Heart* is grateful to you.

Days

Prayer on Waking

God of Creation,
Grant me a gentle day,
A kind and a sweet day,
A day of light and breath,
A day of love and service.

Holy One,
Thank You for renewing me to life,
For restoring my soul to my body
And for returning me—in joy and gratitude—
To Your gifts and blessings.

Meditation for Today

God,
Help me through this day.
Guide me toward kindness, gentleness, and peace.
Grant me strength and endurance,
Courage and humor,
So that I may do Your will with a full heart,
In joy and in love.
Grant me wholeness,
A day filled with wonder and awe.
Then, God of all being,
I will become a source of blessings,
A bearer of Your light in the world.

Modeh/Modah Ani

מוֹדֶה\מוֹדָה אֲנִי לְפָנֶיךָ,
מֶלֶךְ חַי וְקַיָּם,
שֶׁהֶחֱזַרְתָּ בִּי נִשְׁמָתִי בְּחֶמְלָה,
רַבָּה אֱמוּנָתֶךָ.

Modeh/modah ani l'fanecha,
Melech chai v'kayam,
she-hechezarta bi nishmati b'chemlah,
rabbah emunatecha.

I thank You, God,
Creator of life, Eternal One,
For restoring my soul to me with love
Filled with Your eternal trust.

I thank You, God,
Creator of life, Eternal One,
For restoring my love with trust
Filled with Your eternal hope.

I thank You, God,
Creator of life, Eternal One,
For restoring my trust with hope
Filled with Your eternal kindness.

I thank You, God,
Creator of life, Eternal One,
For restoring my hope with kindness
Filled with Your eternal justice.

[*continued*]

I thank You, God,
Creator of life, Eternal One,
For restoring my kindness with justice
Filled with Your eternal mercy.

I thank You, God,
Creator of life, Eternal One,
For restoring my justice with mercy
Filled with Your eternal peace.

I thank You, God,
Creator of life, Eternal One,
For restoring my mercy with peace
Filled with Your eternal soul.

I thank You, God,
Creator of life, Eternal One,
For restoring my peace with soul
Filled with Your eternal love.

I thank You, God,
Creator of life, Eternal One,
For restoring my soul with love
Filled with Your eternal trust.

Prayer of Joy

God,
Thank You for joy and delight,
For wonder and awe,
For moments of gladness and celebration.
Grant me the ability to breathe gentleness
Into my hours and seasons,
So that I live awake to beauty,
To holiness,
To the radiance that surrounds us.
Grant me the wisdom to arrive each day
With passion and humor,
With song and dance,
With smiling eyes,
In service to myself,
In service to others,
In service to Your holy name.

Praise the New Day

Praise the new day,
A gift of the Source of all being,
The Breath of life,
The Soul of the universe.
Let us cherish the moments
And sanctify the hours,
Blessing joys,
Honoring the tears,
Lifting our hearts in song,
Raising our voices in thanksgiving.
To magnify faith
And practice acceptance.
To offer consolation
And to seek wisdom.
To become a well of healing,
A beacon of kindness,
A source of forgiveness,
A light of wonder and wisdom.

Soul of the universe,
Breath of life,
Source of all being,
We praise the new day.
A gift of holiness and love.

Morning Blessings

Blessed are You, Adonai our God, Sovereign of the universe . . .

> . . . Who created a world of luminous wonder.
> . . . Who created a world of radiant splendor.
> . . . Who created a world of shimmering glory.
> . . . Source of life and health.
> . . . Well of joy and love.
> . . . Fountain of forgiveness and hope.
> . . . Who grants rest and renewal.
> . . . Who grants strength and fortitude.
> . . . Who grants wisdom and understanding.
> . . . Who delights in prayer.
> . . . Who delights in service.
> . . . Who delights in righteousness.

Blessed are You, Adonai our God, Sovereign of the universe,
Creator of this new day, Source of sustenance,
Bless the works of my hands so that I become
A source of holiness and healing.

Meditation at Noon

There's still time to live this day with intention,
To set aside petty thoughts and small tasks,
To regard myself with dignity and grace.

There's still time to live this day with my hands
    and my heart,
To walk with strength,
To act with courage,
To offer kindness,
To build and to sustain,
To embrace and to bless.

God of forgiveness,
Thank You for the gift of hope
That You've planted in every moment,
The gift of renewal that You've given to every hour,
So that we may find the way
To redeem our days with holiness.

Your Name: Meditation at Dusk

God of our ancestors,
Your name is Peace.
Your name is Justice.
Your name is Mercy.

God of life,
Your name is Compassion.
Your name is Love.
Your name is Hope.

God of blessing,
Your name is Truth.
Your name is Wisdom.
Your name is Righteousness.

God of our fathers,
God of our mothers,
Your name is in my heart
And before my eyes.

Blessed are You, Adonai,
Your name shines throughout Creation.

Evening Blessings

Blessed are You, Adonai our God, Sovereign of the universe,
Who has given me the . . .

> . . . gifts of the body.
> . . . delights of the senses.
> . . . beauty of the heart.
> . . . dignity of the mind.
> . . . radiance of the soul.
> . . . mystery of the spirit.
> . . . blessings of Your word.
> . . . majesty of Your wisdom.
> . . . presence of Your glory.
> . . . wonder of being.

Blessed are You, Adonai our God, Sovereign of the universe,
For these and all Your gifts, we sanctify and praise Your
holy name.

Meditation at Night

God of mystery,
Thank You for the gift of this day,
For the one ending,
And the one about to begin.
Help me to see the moments and the hours,
Those already past and those to come,
As blessings, as teachers.
Guide me to service for Your name's sake.
Grant me comfort and rest
So that I enter the new day
With a sense of joy, hope, and peace.
Then, God of old,
I will become a source of love,
A beacon of wonder, awe, and grace.

Prayer before Sleep

God,
Watch over my sleep.
Grant me a night of rest and renewal,
And spread Your loving shelter
Over my family and friends,
My [wife/husband/partner/child(ren)/mother/father]
And all who are dear to me.
Keep us safe throughout the night
And stay present when the morning comes.
This night I'm keenly aware of those in special need
of Your care.

Ancient One,
Ease my mind,
Soothe my heart,
Rejuvenate my body,
Restore my strength,
Revive my faith,
So that when I open my eyes
To the new day
I will see beauty in Your Creation
And marvel in all Your works.
Then, I will rise
In service to Torah and mitzvot,
In service to Your will,
A testimony to Your holy name.

Birdsong at Midnight

Sometimes a bird will sing at midnight.
Perhaps restless, perhaps confused,
Perhaps so full of joy and love
That music bursts forth.

Fill me with song on sleepless nights.
Fill me with music in the lonely deep.
Let the promise of a new day
Bring comfort and consolation.

An Amazing Life

This is an amazing life,
A gift of moments
Precious and dear,
Profound in joy,
Profound in sorrow.

This is an amazing life,
A gift of moments
Glorious and holy,
Rich in laughter,
Rich with tears.

This is an amazing life,
A gift, a song,
A fantastic story of solitude and adventure,
A tale of darkness and light,
A psalm of frailty and endurance,
A poem written in time and motion,
In stillness and silence,
In shouts and whispers,
In mourning and wondrous celebration.

This is an amazing life,
A river of blessings,
A gift to cherish
In awe and wonder.
Blessed are the gifts of life.
Blessed is the Giver of life.
Blessed is this amazing life.

Seasons

For Spring

Shimmering, radiant air
Alive with new warmth.
Sunshine waking the earth,
Calling the grasses to grow
And bulbs to prepare flowers.
Winds clear the remnants of seasons past,
Old leaves and dry branches,
Making way for new life.
And the rain joins the sun to feed the land.
Bless this day, God of seasons.
Bless the spring with energy and hope.
Be present with us as we celebrate the glory of Creation,
Planting the land and our lives with Your gifts,
These gardens of holiness and love.

God of time and space,
May this season be a blessing and a teacher.
Make me like the sunshine, a source of light.
Make me like the earth, flowing with bounty, ready to give.
Bless my days with service and my nights with peace.
Make me like a garden,
A source of beauty and purpose,
Sustenance and splendor.

For Summer

Heat and light,
Day overtakes night,
Warm air settles over the earth,
The land vibrant with growth.
Your creatures build and thrive.
Mornings, alive with motion,
As warmth surrenders to heat.
Nights, bursting forth with wonder.
Bless this day, God of seasons,
Bless the summer with energy and vitality,
So that all of Your creatures
Enter the coming seasons
In the fullness of Your bounty.

God of time and space,
May this season be a blessing and a teacher.
Make me like the land,
Fertile with sustenance and beauty.
Make me like the midnight sky,
Sparkling with ancient gifts.
Bless my days with service
And my evenings with rest.
Make me like the summer dawn,
Vibrant, awake, vital, and ready.

For Autumn

The rains have come,
Windy days and crisp nights.
Days are shorter now
As the land prepares to sleep.
Bless this day, God of seasons.
Bless the autumn with the hope of comfort and rest.
Be present with us as we gather with family and friends
So that we enliven our moments with love and joy.

God of time and space,
May this season be a blessing and a teacher.
Make me like the coming rain, nourishing all that I touch.
Make me like a gentle wind, quietly clearing old habits
And the debris of my mistakes.
Make me like the crisp air,
Present, refreshing, and free.
Bless my days with service and my nights with prayer.
Make me like the land, seeking solace and rest.

For Winter

Cold and dark,
Night overtakes day,
Frigid air settles over the earth.
The land waits while Your creatures rest.
Then, a shift.
Small, imperceptible,
The days slowly lengthen
And mornings surrender to light.
Bless this day, God of seasons.
Bless the winter with rest, renewal, and love.
Be present with us as we prepare
For another cycle of seasons
With dignity and purpose.

God of time and space,
May this season be a blessing and a teacher.
Make me like the long, deep night,
A blanket of solace and comfort.
Make me like the returning sun,
A source of quiet hope.
Bless my days with service and my nights with warmth.
Make me like a new day
Dawning from the darkness.

For Rain

Source of life and blessings,
The rains come in their seasons
To feed the land, the crops, the gardens.
The earth abundant, food plentiful, gardens lush.
Sweet, clean water, feeding rivers, filling the sea.
Sometimes too much,
Sometimes too little,
Sometimes not at all.

Fountain of blessing,
Remember us with life,
With beauty,
With prosperity and bounty.
Remember us with the gift of rain,
The gifts of earth and sky,
Blessings upon the land,
Each in its time,
Each in its season,
Each in its proper measure.

Come, Rain

Come, rain,
Pour forth
Upon this barren land,
Upon this barren heart.
The earth is dry,
My chest is withered,
And love has fled
For more fertile ground.

Come, rain,
Pour forth
With abandon,
Fill the air with moisture,
Feed the ground with promise,
Let living water
Soak through me,
A gift of heaven,
A gift of holiness,
A fountain of glory,
A well of healing,
A source of power,
Pounding through my thirsty veins.

Harvest Prayer

The yield arrives
Full and ripe,
Plump and ready,
Bursting in flavor,
Brimming with gifts
Of earth and sky.
Tree and grass,
Vine and root,
Blessings of the rich soil,
The gentle rain,
The constant sun.
Blessings from the flow of seasons,
And the labor of our hands.
Blessings of abundance and grace,
The work of Your Creation.

Blessed are You, Adonai our God,
Source of life,
Your bounty sustains us.

Shabbat

For the Arrival of Shabbat

Well of life,
Bless my heart with the gifts of Shabbat,
The presence of Your love in my pulse,
Your glory in my chest,
And Your wonder in my breath.
Bless my eyes with the gifts of Shabbat,
The beauty of the candlesticks,
The *Kiddush* cups and challot.
Bless my lips with the gifts of Shabbat,
Rejoicing in song and prayer,
Our melodies ancient and new.
Bless my ears with the gifts of Shabbat,
Hymns and praises,
The *nigunim* of old,
And blessed words of Torah.
Bless my soul with the gifts of Shabbat,
Awe and thanksgiving,
Calm and surrender,
Beauty, righteousness, and peace.

Let these gifts descend gently on all Your people Israel,
So that together,
Wherever we may be,
In one voice
From the four corners of earth we sing,

בּוֹאֲכֶם לְשָׁלוֹם,
מַלְאֲכֵי הַשָּׁלוֹם,
מַלְאֲכֵי עֶלְיוֹן.

Bo-achem l'shalom
Malachei hashalom,
Malachei elyon.

Come in peace,
Messengers of peace,
Angels of the Most High.

Come, Beloved

If you listen,
Listen.
If you listen you will hear
Shabbat descend from her distant place,
Gently clearing the air
Of the steady buzz of the mundane,
Gently inviting you to stillness,
Gently preparing the space
For the arrival of holiness.

If you listen,
Listen.
If you listen you will hear
The arrival of luminous wonder,
A radiance of glory that touches your heart,
So that love pulses through your veins.
The gates of your soul burst open,
You run through them, skipping, singing,
מַהֵר אָהוּב
Maheir ahuv,
Hurry, beloved . . .
How long since your hands touched mine,
How long since your lips brushed
These tired eyes,
How long since I rested in you.

[*continued*]

כִּי בָא מוֹעֵד
Ki va mo-eid,
For the time has come,
The time has come to reunite.
And tears of surrender,
Shimmering with the taste of honey,
Will pour through you like grace from God's ancient well.
וְחָנֵּנוּ כִּימֵי עוֹלָם
V'choneini kimei olam.

If you listen,
Listen.
Listen . . .

Sowing Light

Light is sown by the righteous,
Tucked into cracks in the sidewalks,
Dropped in the grass,
Breathed into the air,
Left waiting for others to find.

You who are upright in heart,
Let your deeds declare your love,
Let your hands be a source of healing,
Let your joy be a fountain of blessing.

Rejoice in righteousness,
And spread holiness throughout your days.
Light is sown for you.
Seek it,
Find it,
Magnify it
In service to God's holy name.

Shabbat Settles on Jerusalem

Shabbat settles on Jerusalem
Like a dove,
Gliding on silent wings.

Shabbat settles in my heart,
A lover with open arms,
Embracing my soul with song,
Wrapped in quiet breathing.

I send blessings into the world.
Light.
Bread.
Prayers of peace.

Sephardi Quarter Note

If you listen
To the space between
The notes and the half notes,
The space between heartbeats,
You'll hear quarter notes of love and yearning,
Ancient music of hope and sorrow,
Infinite in variation,
The echo of generations.
Notes that bend toward God.
Notes that linger with longing.
Notes that plead for redemption.
Notes that declare:
"Torah is my life and mitzvot are my honor."
Notes that proclaim:
"I am waiting for you, God of Abraham."
Notes of surrender.
Notes that refuse to surrender.
Notes that cry out to Zion and Israel.
The voice of sorrow
And the voice of laughter.

If you listen
To the space between
The notes and the half notes,
The rises and the falls,
The trills and trumpets,
You will hear a rhythm and a pulse
Calling out:

[*continued*]

"אֲדוֹן עוֹלָם
יְדִיד נֶפֶשׁ
שַׁחַר אֲבַקֶשְׁךָ
יוֹדְךָ רְעֵיוֹנַי
Adon Olam,
Yedid Nefesh,
Shachar Avakeshcha,
Yodukha Rayonai.
Master of the Universe,
Beloved of my Heart,
At Dawn I Seek You,
My Thoughts will Praise You."

In the space between the notes,
Dreams of God
Touch the core of being
To become music.

About Shabbat

Majestic Sovereign,
Well of blessings,
How did You decide
To create heaven and earth?
Was this Your purpose:
To make a world of work,
For us to toil in service?
Did You bring forth a day of rest
As a gift to Your Creation?
Or was this Your only option,
After first conceiving
The glory of Shabbat?
Was the Sabbath itself
Your only intention?
Perhaps You summoned
Time and space
Solely to bring forth
The magnificent splendor
Of Shabbat.

Shabbat Blessing for Children Who Have Left Home

My children,
Dear ones,
You are distant but present,
Your faces shining in my heart,
Lights before my eyes.

Bless you on your journey.
Bless you in your home and on your travels.
May you be surrounded with
Joy and beauty,
Friendship and laughter,
Adventure and wonder,
Hope and love.
Let Torah and mitzvot guide your steps.
[Bless your family.]
[Heal your body and spirit.]
Let God's goodness rain down upon you
From this Shabbat until the next,
And all the days of your life.

Blessing for a Spouse/Partner

Holiness walks with you,
My beloved.
Your face glows,
Your eyes shine,
And beauty surrounds you.
You sparkle with joy and hope.
Your countenance shimmers with the wonder
    of Creation.
You bless the hours and the days.

Let the glory of heaven light your path.
May you know God's blessing
And God's shelter,
Even as you fill our lives with strength and purpose,
With Torah and mitzvot,
With Shabbat and holy days,
With your radiance,
And with your love.

A Shabbat Blessing for Myself

God of rest,
Thank You for the week that has passed.
Thank You for this Shabbat.
Bless those around me with
Your love and Your light.
Let it shine on me, as well.
Help me to live a life of kindness and service
Guided by Torah and mitzvot.
Let me see others through Your eyes,
With compassion and understanding.
Let me see myself through Your eyes,
With forgiveness and grace.
May Your goodness rain down upon me,
From this Shabbat until the next,
And upon those I love,
And all the days of our lives.

Shabbat Is the Place

Shabbat is the place
Where time and space meet,
Without questioning
How the beginning began
Or how the ending ends.

Shabbat is the place
Where song and silence meet,
Blessing each other
With the gift of rest.

Shabbat is the place
Where dreams and angels meet,
Yearning together
For a world of peace.

Shabbat is the place
Where holiness and eternity meet,
Praying together
For the world-to-come.

Farewell, Beloved: A Havdalah Meditation

If you listen,
Listen . . .
If you listen you will hear
Shabbat returning to her distant place,
Retreating slowly, quietly,
Gently opening the space
Between the *kodesh* and the *chol,*
Between the holy and the routine,
Separating eternity from the ordinary.

If you listen you will hear
The music of Shabbat rise,
Leaving behind the scent
Of cinnamon, cardamom, and cloves,
A taste of sweet wine,
A braided beam from beyond time,
A memory and a promise.

לַיְהוּדִים הָיְתָה אוֹרָה וְשִׂמְחָה וְשָׂשׂוֹן וִיקָר . . .
La-Y'hudim hay'tah orah v'simchah v'sason vikar . . .
We once had light and gladness,
Joy and honor . . .
May it return.

בִּמְהֵרָה בְיָמֵינוּ, יָבוֹא אֵלֵינוּ . . .
Bimheirah v'yameinu, yavo eileinu . . .
Come speedily, in our time,
Bringing blessings of peace,
A world of wholeness,
When beauty and wonder,
Justice and mercy,
Kindness and love
Reign on earth.

Jewish Holy Days

For Creation

Author of life,
Architect of Creation,
Artist of earth,
Your works declare Your holy name.

Mighty rivers,
Turbulent seas,
Towering mountains,
Rolling hills,
Vast spaces of brilliance and grandeur.

You created pallet and paint,
Color and hue,
Shape and form,
Abundant and beautiful,
Glorious and majestic,
Full of mystery and wonder.

Blessed are You,
With divine love You created a world of splendor.

Sweet Cake

Give me a drop of honey,
And I will give you the harvest moon.
Give me a silent tear,
And I will give you the roaring sea.
Give me a cup of milk,
And I will give you the rising sun.
Give me your secret prayer,
And I will give you my broken heart.

Give me a drop of honey,
And we will make a feast of this life.
Sweet cake,
To feed ourselves with joy and love.
Sweet cake,
To feed the world with awe and wonder.
Sweet cake,
Of milk and honey.
Sweet cake,
Of prayers and tears.

The Path of Righteousness

God of what was and what will be,
    Of what might have been and might still be.
God of past and future,
    Of memories and beginnings.
God of the finite and the infinite,
    Of moments and possibilities.
What is my life?
    And what of my death?
What of my choices?
    And what of my future?
What of this distance?
    And what of the endless sky?
What of the darkness?
    And what of the light?

God of the seen and unseen,
    Of the known and unknowable.
Teach me patience and understanding
    As the mysteries of my life unfold.
Teach me to live gently, love generously,
    And to walk with strength and confidence.
Teach me to give and to receive,
    Sharing Your blessings in joy and sorrow.
Teach me to see others through Your eyes,
    As children of God.
And teach me to see myself and my life as You do,
    With love.

Blessed are You, Adonai,
Source of life,
Guardian and Shelter,
You set Your people on the path of righteousness,
Holiness and charity,
Kindness and grace,
To return to You in devoted service.
Blessed is Your holy name.

God's Plan: An Introspection

If God's plan
Followed my plan,
I would have no scars on my skin
Or in my heart.

If God's plan
Followed my plan,
I would not have felt the fire or the ice,
Heard the beauty or the terror,
Seen the new bud or the dying leaf.

If God's plan
Followed my plan,
I would not have learned to grieve or cherish,
To hope or surrender,
To be broken and still be whole.

What, then, keeps me locked in fear,
In dread of yielding to Your great works,
Your awesome love,
Your radiant power?
What small desire,
Petty hope—
What yearning of self—
Blocks my service in God's holy name?

[*continued*]

God on high,
Release me from my judgments and designs.
Open my heart to You fully,
Without reservation.
Cast out my doubts and shames,
So I may receive Your divine wisdom and strength.

God of all being,
Make my limbs Your tools and
My voice Your messenger.
Make my heart Your tabernacle,
A dwelling place of holiness
And splendor.

The Season of Healing

This is the season of healing:
Of healing our hearts and souls,
Of healing the moments we share with each other
And the moments we share with ourselves.

This is the season of memory:
Of remembering our parents and grandparents,
The love of generations,
The holiness of our ancestors.

This is the season of stillness,
The season of silence and quiet:
Of deep breaths,
Of open eyes,
Of compassion and consolation.

This is the season of healing:
The season of grief turning to wonder,
Of loss turning toward hope,
The season that binds this year to the next,
The season that heralds the redemption of spirit
And our return to God's Holy Word.

Cry No More

Cry no more for the sins of the past.
Rejoice in your repentance and your return.
For this is the day God made
To lift you up from your sorrow and shame
To deliver you to the gates of righteousness.

Remember this:
Love is the crown of your life
And wisdom the rock on which you stand.
Charity is your staff
And justice your shield.
Your deeds declare your kindness,
And your works declare your devotion.

Cry no more for your fears and your dread.
Rejoice in your blessings and your healing.
For this is the day God made
To raise your countenance and hope,
To deliver you to the gates of holiness.

Who, Still Broken

Who by fire,
Screaming with seared flesh?
Who by water,
Gasping for one more breath?

Rock of life,
Tell me that these are not
Your tools of justice.
Tell me that these are not
Your verdicts or Your punishments.
How do You bear the cries
Of Your children?
The starving,
The battered,
Buried in rubble
Or washed to sea?

No, this is not my God.
Neither Judge nor Witness,
Prosecutor nor Executioner,
Issuing severe decrees
In a kangaroo court
Of intimidations
And forced confessions.

[*continued*]

כִּי כְשִׁמְךָ כֵּן תְּהִלָּתֶךָ.

Ki k'shimcha kein t'hilatecha.

For according to Your name,

So is Your praise.

Your name is Righteousness. Forgiveness. Love.

Your names are Mother, Father, and Teacher.

Your names are Source and Shelter.

קָשֶׁה לִכְעֹס וְנוֹחַ לִרְצוֹת.

Kasheh lichos v'noach lirtzot.

You are slow to anger

And ready to forgive.

But I,

I am slow to change,

Slow to amend my ways.

I can be consumed by the fire

Of my own anger.

I can drown in the sea

Of my own sorrow.

I need Your guidance,

Your gentle hand.

וְאַתָּה הוּא מֶלֶךְ, אֵל חַי וְקַיָּם.

V'atah hu Melech, El chai v'kayam!

For You are forever our living God and Sovereign!

[*continued*]

Yes, I will fall to my knees
Before You.
For You are holy,
Your Majesty fills the universe.
My origin is dust
And I will return to dust.
Until then,
God of mercy,
תְּשׁוּבָה, תְּפִילָה, וּצְדָקָה
T'shuvah, t'filah, u'tzedakah—
Repentance, prayer, and righteousness—
Will allow me to rise,
To stand before You,
Human,
Humble,
Fallible,
Still broken,
And still whole.

Repentance Inside

This I confess:
I have taken my transgressions with me,
Carrying them year by year into my hours and days,
My lapses of conscience
And indiscretion with words,
My petty judgments
And my vanity,
Clinging to grief and fear, anger and shame,
Clinging to excuses and to old habits.
I've felt the light of heaven,
Signs and wonders in my own life,
And still will not surrender to holiness and light.

God of redemption,
With Your loving and guiding hand
Repentance in prayer is easy.
Repentance inside,
Leaving my faults and offenses behind,
Is a struggle.
In Your wisdom You have given me this choice:
To live today as I lived yesterday,
Or to set my life free to love You,
To love Your people,
And to love myself.

God of forgiveness, help me to leave my
    transgressions behind,
To hear Your voice,
To accept Your guidance,
And to see the miracles in each new day.

Blessed are You,
God of justice and mercy,
You who sets Your people on the road to *t'shuvah*.

Forgiveness Inside

This I confess:
I have locked forgiveness away,
Hiding its wonder and grace
In a secret spot deep in my heart.
I have set myself up as judge and accuser,
As provocateur and jury,
Regarding my own words and deeds,
My wisdom and my truth,
With loathing and with disdain.
I have known forgiveness from God,
But not from myself.

God of redemption,
With Your loving and guiding hand
Seeking forgiveness is easy.
Accepting forgiveness is a struggle.
In Your wisdom You have given me this choice:
To live a life of condemnation,
Or to set my heart free to love You,
To love Your people,
And to love myself.

God of mercy, help me to leave my judgments behind,
To hear Your voice,
To accept Your guidance,
And to see the miracles in each new day.

Blessed are You,
God of righteousness,
In Your wisdom You have taught
That forgiveness is the road to peace.

The Season of Return

This is the season of return:
Of returning to ourselves and to our people,
Of returning to our God
And returning to our calling.

This is the season of quiet:
Of quieting the mind to hear the Voice,
Of quieting the heart to hear the Soul,
Of quieting the self to make space for the *Ein Sof*.

This is the season of surrender:
Of surrendering odd quirks and old habits to dignity
    and kindness,
Of surrendering fear and despair to hope and adventure,
    to honor and service.

This is the season of return:
Of returning to wholeness and love,
To prayer and charity,
To family and friends.
This is the season that reminds us of who we are
And who we might become.
The season that summons us to return ourselves
    to purpose,
And our lives to God's Holy Word.

Beauty Dances

Beauty dances
With us
Whenever we build
A tabernacle
To God's holy name.

Love sings
With us
Whenever we rejoice
In gladness
On God's festive days.

Peace cries
With us
Whenever we yearn
In prayer
For God's holy shelter.

Come,
Let us build this place,
This tabernacle where we praise,
With all of our hearts,
God's pardon and promise.
Let us build this place,
Where we delight,
With thanksgiving and wonder,
In God's bounty and gifts.

[*continued*]

Come,
Let us build this place,
This *sukkat shalom*,
This shelter of peace,
Where beauty dances
And love sings.
Where peace cries out:
Build, build,
You Children of Israel,
A tent of holiness,
Strong and true.
Build it in your heart,
In your home,
In your life,
In God's world.

Rejoice!

Dance one thousand steps toward heaven.
Sing one thousand hymns of praise.
Breathe one thousand breaths of glory.
Rejoice!

Climb one thousand steps of courage.
Chant one thousand hymns of hope.
Laugh one thousand breaths of healing.
Rejoice!

Walk one thousand steps of power.
Hum one thousand hymns of life.
Share one thousand breaths of wonder.
Rejoice!

Leap one thousand steps toward beauty.
Cry one thousand hymns of joy.
Feel one thousand breaths of mystery.
Rejoice! Rejoice!

The Season of Building

This is the season of building:
Of building tents of holiness,
Shelters of peace
In our land and in our hearts.

This is the season of rejoicing:
Of rejoicing in God's bounty and grace,
In the radiance and splendor
In heaven and on earth.

This is the season of thanksgiving:
Of giving thanks for the gifts of the land,
For gifts yet to come
As we delight in the wonders of Creation.

This is the season of building:
The season of building tabernacles of joy and gladness,
In our moments and in our days,
In our homes and in our lives.
This is the season that summons jubilation
    and exultation
As we yearn for the great promise to be fulfilled:
A world of harmony and love
Under one great Sukkah,
A sanctuary of wonder and awe
For all nations and all peoples,
Men and women arrayed in the light of God's glory,
Until the end of days.

Meditation before Taking Down a Sukkah

Source of blessings,
I've/we've served meals,
Hosted guests,
Laughed,
And sung with joy,
Here, in this temporary structure,
Creating sacred space
With hope and love.
This dwelling represents
My/our hope(s) for comfort and shelter,
For wholeness and healing,
A life/lives of song and dance,
Joy and laughter,
Kindness and goodwill.
As I/we dismantle the physical structure,
I/we strengthen my/our resolve
To build a world of justice and peace,
Taking these aspirations into my/our heart(s).

For the Gift of Torah Scholarship

God, we give thanks for the gift of scholarship,
For wisdom, insight, and understanding,
For the gift that unlocks treasures hidden in Your
　Holy Word.
You gave us Torah at Sinai
And righteous men and women as Your messengers,
Revealing divine secrets stage by stage.
Hear this prayer for those who study Talmud and Torah,
Mishnah and Gemara,
Musar, *Zohar*, and *Tanya*,
The lessons of scholars of every generation.
Make their teaching Your vessel.
Let heaven pour beauty into them
So that they overflow with sacred fire
Drawing others to Your Word,
So that when we study Your mysteries,
Our souls turn back to You in joyous reunion.
Together, we offer our learning back to heaven,
And rejoice.

For the Joy of Learning

God, we give thanks for the joy of learning,
For the love of teaching and being taught,
For the gift that connects us to You,
To each other
And to Your Divine Word.
Your wisdom is near to us,
In our hearts and in our mouths,
In our hands and in our lives,
So that we may teach it to each other
With humility and love.
Hear our prayer for those who teach and learn,
Bringing new light to Your people Israel.
Make our moments together a celebration.
Let heaven pour wisdom and strength through them
So that they overflow with enthusiasm and wonder
Drawing others into Your service,
So that when we witness the love of learning
Our souls turn back to You for wisdom.
Together, we offer this journey back to heaven
And rejoice.

Lamps Within

A lamp glows inside your heart,
With eight ways to light it,
Eight ways to keep it shining,
Eight ways to keep its glow.

Light it with your joy.
Light it with your tears.
Light it with this song.
Light it with the works of your hands.
Light it with hope.
Light it with service.
Light it with this prayer.
Light it with praise to God's holy name.

Bring the lamp of your soul out into the street
So that all who have forgotten
The miracles around us
Will remember the beauty within,
So that all who have forgotten
The miracles of old
Will remember and rejoice.

A lamp glows inside your children.
Keep it shining.
Watch it glow.

Light it with your joy.
Light it with your tears.
Light it with this song.
Light it with the works of your hands.
Light it with hope.
Light it with service.
Light it with prayer.
Light it with praise to God's holy name.

The Season of Dedication

This is the season of dedication:
Of dedicating our moments and our lives,
Of dedicating our hope and our strength,
To live by God's Word.

This is the season of cleansing:
Of cleansing our hearts and our sanctuaries,
Of cleansing our deeds and our ways,
Creating sacred time and space.

This is the season of service:
Of service to our neighbors and community,
Of service to *K'lal Yisrael*,
In the name of justice and peace.

This is the season of dedication:
Of dedication to strength and honor,
Righteousness and duty.
This is the season that calls forth miracles,
That summons the light of holiness,
The season that reminds us to rebuild and restore
Our commitment to Torah and mitzvot
In God's holy name.

Egypt Inside

This I confess:
I have taken Egypt with me.
I've kept myself a slave to grief and loss,
Fear and anger and shame.
I have set myself up as taskmaster,
Driving myself beyond the limits
Of reasonable time and common sense.
I've seen miracles from heaven,
Signs and wonders in my own life,
Yet I've taken Egypt with me,
Still waiting for heaven to speak.

God of redemption,
With Your loving and guiding hand leaving Egypt is easy.
Leaving Egypt behind is a struggle.
In Your wisdom You've given me this choice:
To live in a tyranny of my own making,
Or to set my heart free to love You,
To love Your people,
And to love myself.

God of freedom,
Help me to leave Egypt behind,
To hear Your voice,
To accept Your guidance,
And to see the miracles in each new day.

Blessed are You, God of wonder,
You set Your people on the road to redemption.

The Season of Freedom

This is the season of freedom:
Of freedom from the will of tyrants,
Of freedom from the bondage of self,
The freedom to receive God's Holy Word.

This is the season of release:
Of release from captivity and oppression,
Of release from a foreign land,
To become a nation and a people.

This is the season of redemption:
Of redeeming our bodies and souls,
Of redeeming our strength and power,
In service to *Am Yisrael*.

This is the season of freedom:
Of reliving the ancient journey,
Of remembering the treacherous path.
This is the season that calls us to stand together,
The season that summons us to God's Law,
The season that leads us home.

The Season of Counting

This is the season of counting:
Of counting days and nights,
Of counting the space between slavery of the body
And freedom of the soul.

This is the season of seeing:
Of seeing earth and sky,
Of seeing renewal in the land
And renewal in our hearts.

This is the season of journeying:
Of inner journeys and outer journeys
Taking us places that need us,
Places that we need.

This is the season of counting,
The season of joyous anticipation,
Of wondrous waiting,
In devotion and awe,
For our most precious gift,
The gift that binds our hearts to each other across
    the millennia,
The gift that binds our souls to God's Holy Word.

God's Voice

What if God's voice was so near
That your bones rattled
As thunder echoes inside your chest?

What if God's voice was so near
You could feel the wind hit your face
As your feet seem to slip on shaking ground?

What if awe and wonder surrounded you,
So close that your knees buckled,
As a pillar of fire from heaven descends to earth?

What if holiness packed the empty space with light
As your lungs fill with the one divine breath
Together with every other living being?

What if God's voice is as near
As your willingness to remember
The moment we stood together on Sinai,
Amid the smoke and the lightning,
Hearing the great blast of the shofar?

What if that moment
Is now?

God on Tiptoes

What if God arrived unannounced?
No smoke. No thunder.
A gentle appearance of radiance and love.

What if God snuck in on tiptoes?
No earthquake. No blast of the shofar.
A luminous presence of wonder and glory.

What if God's voice whispered in your ear,
So quietly that you had to hold your breath to hear?
A silent surrender of hope and faith.

What if holiness packed the empty space with light
As your lungs filled with the one divine breath
Together with every other living being?

What if God's voice was as near
As your willingness to listen quietly
To the Soul of the universe,
As a sense of calm and peace
Passes through you?

What if that moment
Is now?

Other Special Days

For the New Year

God of time and space,
Source of rhythm and grace,
You've granted me moments and breaths,
Life like a river,
Rapids and flats,
Deep narrow canyons
And bright open skies,
Thundering, churning waters
And calm gentle flows.
A life of beauty and wonder
Beyond my understanding,
Beyond my wildest dreams.
And yet,
And still, Heavenly Redeemer,
You also give me choices.
To live in grief or joy,
Fear or awe,
Tears or laughter.
To lift my life in glory and radiance,
To be a shining light of kindness and love.

Another Year: An Introspection

Another year slips away,
As do they all,
Day by day,
Hour by hour,
Moment by moment.
Many used wisely,
Many wasted.

Another year opens,
As do they all,
With anticipation,
With wonder and amazement,
With excitement,
With consolation.

Was last year so different from the one before?
What will this New Year bring?
What will I bring to this New Year?

This I pledge to myself:
Love is my answer to grief,
Hope is my answer to loss,
Strength is my answer to fear,
Honor is my answer to slander,
Action is my answer to injustice.

This I pledge to you
My sisters and brothers:
To see you as you are,
To respect your journey,
To hear your truth,
To stand with you in dignity,
To walk with you as a companion and friend.

[continued]

This I pledge to You
God of my ancestors:
To seek Your wisdom,
To follow Your command,
To obey Your Law,
To observe Your Sabbath,
To rejoice in Your works,
To do Your will.

God of time and space,
Another year slips away,
As do they all.
Another year opens before me,
As do they all:
With one hundred choices,
One thousand possibilities,
And one sacred duty.
Life. This life. My life.

Let Truth

Let truth shine from your face,
Spark from your eyes,
Overflow from your lips.

Let truth protect your heart,
Shield your lungs,
Exude from your chest.

Let truth strengthen your bones,
Engage your nerves,
Capture your being.

For truth is in each moment and each question,
The earth's hot core and the cold edge of the universe,
The flow of wisdom from God's Holy Word,
Divine mysteries and secrets,
Calling out to you, my sisters and brothers:
  "Awake you slumberers!
   Awake you who sit idle and hapless against the tide
      of dishonesty and deceit.
   Have you forgotten My promises?
   Have you forsaken our covenant, our pact to care
      for Creation?
   Have you turned away from your hopes and ideals?"

[continued]

This, then, is God's command:
Let truth envelop you,
Protect you,
Flow through you.
Let truth carry you into honest days
And righteous seasons.
Speak and teach,
Listen and hear,
Lifting your life with dignity and understanding.
Let truth be your signature and your legacy.

Blessed are You, God of truth.

The Preacher Said

Let us pray,
The preacher said,
Let us pray in the name of hope,
In the name of justice,
In the name of truth.

Let us commit to each other,
The preacher said,
Commit in the name of equality,
In the name of righteousness,
And in the name of our children.

Let us take to the streets,
The preacher said,
Let us take to the streets
To make our space,
To claim a place,
For no one race
Can live in grace,
Until we face,
Together,
Oppression and hate.

[continued]

Let us walk,
The preacher said,
Let us walk from Selma to Montgomery,
From oppression to the Promised Land,
From fear to courage,
From silence to action,
From today to the future,
To a place where all people
Will be judged by the content
Of their character,
The humanity of their words,
And the compassion of their deeds.

Stick with love,
The preacher said,
Stick with love
Because love is the only answer.

Stick with love.
Stick with love.

Let us pray,
The preacher said,
Let us pray in the name of hope,
In the name of justice,
In the name of truth.

Against Worker Exploitation

God of the laborer,
God of the migrant and the ensnared,
The voices of the misused echo across the land,
Overworked and undervalued in the name of profit.
Our children,
Our brothers,
And our sisters
Toil in misery,
Chained to taskmasters
By slavery, poverty, or misfortune.
Bound to unbearable hours
And cruel conditions
So that others may reap the rewards
Of their suffering and endurance.

Source of abundance and grace,
Creator of affluence and wealth,
You call upon us to stand in the name of justice
    and fairness,
To witness against the abuse of economic power,
To fight corporate neglect of human beings,
To battle against theft at the hand of dominance
    and clout.

Bless those who dedicate their lives to the voiceless
    and the forgotten,
Those who work to expose greed and callousness in field
    and factory.
Give them courage and determination.

[*continued*]

Bless those who plead on behalf of the oppressed and
    the subjugated
Before the seats of power,
Governments and corporations.
Give them wisdom and skill.
May their work never falter
Nor despair deter them from this holy calling.

Bless those in financial bondage with new resources.
Release them from want.
Hasten the day of their self-sufficiency and bounty.

Blessed are You, God of all being,
Who summons us to oppose oppression.

Gratitude for Work

God on high,
I'm grateful for the opportunity to work,
To contribute,
To provide for my well-being
[And the well-being of my family].
Let me use this gift for good,
In service to others
And Your holy name.

Remember the poor and the homeless,
The needy and the unemployed,
So that they may find dignity and fulfillment
In the works of their hands
And the works of their minds.
Rescue them from the shadow of fear.
Bless all who are jobless with a livelihood
So that they may know health and happiness,
Security and peace.

Source of goodness and life,
Grant me success and prosperity in all my endeavors.
Grant me the ongoing joy of fruitful labor.

This Bounty

God of abundance,
You have blessed me
With Your bounty
Your love,
Your grace,
The treasures of Your Creation.

In gratitude for these gifts,
Holy One,
Bless me with wisdom
To use them with skill,
In service to Your holy name.

Bless me with humility
To use them with joy,
In service to Your Creation.

Bless me with a generous heart
And a forgiving hand,
In service to Your commandments.

Bless me with a strong arm
And a curious mind,
In the service of *tikkun olam*.

Bless me with gentle speech
And joyous laughter,
So that all my works
Summon holiness into Your world.

Then, Rock of Israel,
I will honor Your glorious gifts
With all my being.

Blessed are You, Adonai our God,
Your bounty calls us to service.

Meditation at the Thanksgiving Table

God on high,
What an abundance of gifts
Arrayed before us.
Food, family, friends.
Your bounty and grace.

Let us remember those in need
And those represented here in silence:
The fruit and vegetables picked by migrant workers.
The fields planted and picked by underpaid laborers
In the cold rain and blazing sun.
The clothing made by children in factories,
Modern-day slaves indentured by poverty.

Let me remember those who suffer daily
Alone and in fear.
Perhaps someone at this table or in a home nearby
Is nursing a broken heart,
Or hiding the secret of addiction, violence, trauma,
    or pain,
Whose sorrows and losses are often judged and shunned
By our neighbors and our society.

Let this day be the beginning of a deeper love for
    all beings.
Let this day be the beginning of healing for all creatures.
Let this day be the foundation of service to Your world.
Let this moment be for rejoicing in all Your gifts.

[*continued*]

Thank You,
God on high,
For the gifts placed before us:
The awareness of suffering and
The opportunity to heal,
The abundance in our lives and
Your call to share these riches
In love.

Giving Thanks

To whom shall I give this grateful heart,
This joy that shines through the center of my being?
  To you, my friends,
    Who hold me, support me, and carry me along the way.
  To You, my God,
    Source of strength and hope.

To whom shall I give these praising lips,
This gladness that echoes from the depths of my voice?
  To you, my friends,
    Who teach me, guide me, and honor me along the way.
  To You, my God,
    Source of wisdom and truth.

To whom shall I give these powerful hands,
This energy that infuses my bones and sinews?
  To you, my friends.
    Together we will build this world into a temple of
      justice and peace.
  To You, my God.
    Together we will bring the light of holiness and love.

Blessed are you, my friends,
In our moments of celebration together
And our moments of service to each other.
Blessed are You, God of all being,
Source of my life,
Creator of joy and gratitude.

Veterans Day Prayer

God of compassion,
God of dignity and strength,
Watch over our veterans
In recognition of their loyal service to this nation.
Bless them with wholeness and love.
Shelter them.
Heal their wounds.
Comfort their hearts.
Grant them peace.

God of justice and truth,
Rock of our lives,
Bless our veterans,
These men and women of courage and valor,
With a deep and abiding understanding
Of our profound gratitude.
Protect them and their families from loneliness
    and want.
Grant them lives of joy and bounty.
May their dedication and honor
Be remembered as a blessing
From generation to generation.

Blessed are You,
Protector and Redeemer,
Our Shield and our Stronghold.

To the Soldier, To the Veteran

These things I do not know:
    The sound of a bullet.
    The power of a blast.
    The blood of a comrade.
    The depth of your wound.
    The terror at midnight.
    The dread at dawn.
    Your fear or your pain.

These things I know:
    The sound of your honor.
    The power of your courage.
    The blood of your wound.
    The depth of your strength.
    The terror that binds you.
    The dread that remains.
    Your dignity and your valor.

For these things we pray:
    The sound of your laughter.
    The power of your voice.
    The blood of your yearning.
    The depth of your healing.
    The joy that frees you.
    The hope that remains.
    Your wholeness and your love.

The Last Soldier

When the last soldier passes on,
When armies are disbanded and militias discharged,
When weapons are abandoned and armor discarded,
Your mission will, at last, be over.

For You know the soldier's secret.
Yours was not a mission of war
Nor a mission of ruin.
Yours was not a mission of destruction
Nor a mission of death.
Your mission was safety, security, protection.
Your mission was honor, loyalty, service.
Your mission was an end to violence, tyranny, despair.

When the last soldier passes on,
When the uniforms are retired and the final grave filled,
We will remember all who served and sacrificed for
  our nation.

Until then, God of mercy,
Watch over our soldiers and our veterans.
Renew their courage.
Rebuild their strength.
Heal their wounds.
Bind their hearts with Your steadfast love.
Remember them,
Bless them,
Sustain them,
And give them peace.

Yizkor for a Soldier

God of the selfless,
God of the strong and the brave,
Grant a perfect rest among the souls of the righteous
To _____ [name],
My [father / mother / sister / brother / child / wife / husband /
    partner / dear one / friend]
Who died in service to our country during the
    _____ [name of war or conflict].
May his/her dedication serve as a shining lamp of
    courage and love.
May her/his memory be sanctified with joy and love.

Bless the souls of all who have died in the name of liberty
and democracy,
Soldiers and veterans,
Civilians and professionals,
Men and women who answered the call of honor and duty.
May their souls be bound up in the bond of life,
A living blessing in our midst.

Turning Points

On Handing Down a Jewish Heirloom

Dear _____,
At this moment/time/season of your _____ [event],
I/we bequeath this _____ [item]
To you as a symbol of my/our love for you
And in the hope that it will keep you connected to our
    history and our heritage.
This _____ [item] was _____ [background of the heirloom].

May this moment be the beginning of a miraculous
    journey.
May this _____ [item] become a cherished symbol
    of your Jewish life,
A reminder of our family's devotion to you,
A reminder of this special day/season.
May it be God's will that one day
You pass it to the next generation, in love.

God of our fathers and mothers,
Bless my/our _____
    [identify the relationship, such as daughter, grandson, niece]
With health and prosperity
Wisdom and happiness,
A life of blessings and peace.
How splendid is this moment!
How amazing in beauty, hope, and joy!
My heart is full.

בָּרוּךְ אַתָּה, יי אלהינו, מֶלֶךְ הָעוֹלָם,
שֶׁהֶחֱיָנוּ וְקִיְּמָנוּ וְהִגִּיעָנוּ לַזְּמַן הַזֶּה.
Baruch atah, Adonai Eloheinu, Melech haolam
shehecheyanu v'kiy'manu v'higianu laz'man hazeh.
Our praise to You, Adonai our God, Sovereign of all,
who has kept us alive, sustained us, and brought us
    to this season.

On Handing Down an Heirloom Tallit at a Bar/Bat Mitzvah

Dear _____,

At this moment of your bar/bat mitzvah

I/we bequeath this tallit to you as a symbol of my/our
 pride in you

And in the hope that it will keep you connected to our
 history and our heritage.

This tallit was _____ [*background of the tallit*].

May this moment be the beginning of a miraculous journey.

May this tallit become a cherished symbol of your
 Jewish life.

My prayer is that each time you put it on

You remember our family's devotion to you,

That you remember this special moment,

And you remember the Jewish call to heal the world.

May it be God's will that one day

You pass this tallit to the next generation, in love.

God of our fathers and mothers,

Bless my/our _____

 [*identify the relationship, such as daughter, grandson, niece*]

With health and prosperity,

Wisdom and happiness,

A life of blessings and peace.

How splendid is this moment!

How amazing in beauty, trust, and joy!

My heart is full.

בָּרוּךְ אַתָּה, יי אלהינו, מֶלֶךְ הָעוֹלָם,
שֶׁהֶחֱיָנוּ וְקִיְּמָנוּ וְהִגִּיעָנוּ לַזְּמַן הַזֶּה.

*Baruch atah, Adonai Eloheinu, Melech haolam
shehecheyanu v'kiy'manu v'higianu laz'man hazeh.*

Our praise to You, Adonai our God, Sovereign of all,

who has kept us alive, sustained us, and brought us
 to this season.

Meditation for a Child's First Torah Reading

Holy One,
Ancient Source of wisdom and truth,
My daughter/son is about to enter
The sacred garden of Your Law,
Chanting Torah on behalf of our people for the first time.
How splendid is this moment!
How full of beauty and hope!
May this be the beginning of a miraculous journey,
A sacred romance of head and heart
Between my daughter/son and the wisdom of the ages,
Between my child and Your Holy Word.
Grant me the ability to listen and to hear
As she/he gives voice to Your mysteries.
May this moment herald a life
Dedicated to unlocking the secrets
Hidden in our holy texts.

God of our mothers and fathers,
May I be privileged to hear her/him
Read Torah again and again,
Always remembering my joy in this moment,
My heart full of praise.

בָּרוּךְ אַתָּה, יי אלהינו, מֶלֶךְ הָעוֹלָם,
שֶׁהֶחֱיָנוּ וְקִיְּמָנוּ וְהִגִּיעָנוּ לַזְּמַן הַזֶּה.

Baruch atah, Adonai Eloheinu, Melech haolam
shehecheyanu v'kiy'manu v'higianu laz'man hazeh.

Our praise to You, Adonai our God, Sovereign of all,
who has kept us alive, sustained us, and brought us
   to this season.

My Child Leaves Home (A Parent's Prayer)

Holy One,
Heavenly Guide,
My daughter/son is leaving home
To begin the adventure of an independent life.
Bless her/his journey with joy and wonder.
Let opportunity open like a rose before her/his eyes.
Be her/his compass and her/his shield.
Lead her/him on a path of discovery
Guided by the love of Torah,
A commitment to mitzvot,
And dedication to the Jewish people.
Bless her/him with mentors and teachers,
Companions and friends,
Scholars and rabbis,
To support and guide her/him along the way.

In this marvel,
In this glorious moment of growth fulfilled,
My heart struggles with contradictions:
Pride and fear,
Joy and grief,
Love and loss.
The landscape of my life is shifting,
Offering new challenges and new choices
In the very moment my child departs.
Give me the wisdom and the strength to honor my own life
With gentleness and courage
And to embrace the beauty and promise of the time
    to come.

[*continued*]

God of our fathers and mothers,
God of sacred transitions,
Bless my daughter/son
_____ [*child's name in Hebrew or your native tongue*]
As she/he sets out on this new stage of life.
Keep her/him safe under the canopy of peace.
And lead her/him back home to me often
With stories of marvelous moments and amazing discovery.

Blessed are You, Adonai our God,
Who watches over the lives of our children.

Bind Our Hearts—A Wedding Prayer

Hope and love,
Love and promise,
Promise and commitment,
Commitment and action,
A sacred pairing,
A holy union,
A celebration of life.

Let this cup of sweetness overflow
Into God's glorious handiwork
As we delight in Creation,
Seeing the divine in each other,
Sharing this abundance with the generations
As loving companions and dedicated friends,
Rejoicing together now and forever.

Bind our hearts with awe,
Bind our hearts with wonder,
Grant us wisdom and understanding,
Patience and forgiveness,
Days of radiance and light,
Nights of comfort and peace,
Lives of blessing.

Affirmation of Faith

Hear O Israel,
>The covenant we made
>Together on Sinai
>Is a pledge for all time,
>A vow for the ages,
>To do and to listen,
>To teach and to learn
>With the fullness of our hearts,
>From the depths of our souls
>And the strength of our being,
>Binding ourselves to

Adonai our God
>With Torah and mitzvot,
>Binding our lives to each other
>With righteousness and charity,
>So that blessings will rain down from heaven
>To feed our hearts and fill our land
>With God's abundant gifts,
>The brilliance and wonder
>That flow from service to God's Holy Word,
>In remembrance of Creation
>And our liberation from slavery,
>Declaring throughout the generations:

God is One,
>God is One,
>God is One.

שְׁמַע יִשְׂרָאֵל יְיָ אלהינו יְיָ אֶחָד!

Sh'ma Yisrael, Adonai Eloheinu, Adonai Echad!

Hear, O Israel! Adonai is our God! Adonai is One!

For Pregnancy

God of our mothers,
My yearning is as old as creation,
As old as love,
As old as life.

Bless my body with the wonders of pregnancy
And my days with the promise of birth.
Bless my heart with the gift of a child,
And my soul with the gift of hope,
The gift of generations.

God of Mercy,
My yearning is as fresh as dew,
Ripe with longing,
Ripe with desire.
Hear my voice.
[Hear my grief.]
Hear my prayer.

Blessed are You,
Source of life.

For Fertility Treatment (Women)

God of Mercy,
I have prayed,
I have cried,
I have shown my sorrow to heaven,
In the name of fulfilling Your command,
In the name of fulfilling my birthright.
Mother.
Vessel of life.
Vessel of love.
Source of joy.
Source of generations.

Rock of Ages,
Has my body betrayed me?
Are my hopes and dreams
Empty, barren, lost?
Grant me courage and fortitude
As I begin/continue fertility treatments.
Grant my doctors wisdom
And my body strength,
So that I may know the holiness and wonder,
The radiance and light,
Of carrying life and giving birth,
In the fullness of health,
In the fullness of joy,
With awe and thanksgiving,
With gratitude and humility,
In service to Your Holy Name.

For Fertility Treatment (Men)

God of our fathers,
God of generations,
How strange is this feeling?
How odd to hear that
My body and my seed are weak,
That I need medical help to fulfill my duty,
My honor, my joy,
Of partnership in creating a child.

Rock of Ages,
Grant me courage and fortitude
As I begin/continue fertility treatments.
Grant my doctors wisdom
And my body strength,
So that I my know the wonder of fatherhood,
The holiness, radiance, and light
Of bringing life.
Grant me/us a child
In the fullness of health,
In the fullness of joy,
With awe and thanksgiving,
With gratitude and humility,
In service to Your Holy Name.

In Praise of Adoption

God of mercy,
Source of love and shelter,
Bless those who embrace children as their own,
Opening their lives and their hearts
With compassion and care,
Healing the world one small soul at a time,
Men and women with generous hearts
And tender souls.
Bless their lives with wisdom and strength,
Kindness and care,
So that all of their children
Will be nurtured, protected, and educated
With joy and wonder.
Bless these families with health and safety,
Happiness and well-being.

Source of life,
Bless those who hope to adopt,
Those who've waited and yearned
As the adoption process moves slowly, step-by-step.
Let the loving hand of adoption bring their lives
The richness of family / a growing family,
The joys and challenges of parenting.
Bless, too, those who work and advocate
For children and for adoption.
May their energy and effort
Be a source of healing.

Holy One,
Bring the day when all children will know
The love of parents and the joy of family.
For wholeness.
For healing.
For peace.

This Ring: An Ending

When I put this ring on my finger
I wrapped it around my heart.

In removing this ring from my finger
I release my heart
With grief and joy,
Uncertainty and faith,
In unequal measures.

Ancient One,
God of compassion and grace,
Let this moment be a blessing
So that healing continues
To flow into my hours and days.
Grant me the strength and insight
To honor the past and embrace the future
With dignity and passion,
Wisdom and thanksgiving,
Kindness and charity.
Then, God of wholeness and healing,
I will return to song and dance,
Laughter and praise,
As a beacon of Your light,
A source of joy, hope, and love.

End of Life

End-of-Life Vidui

God of our mothers and fathers,
Here I recall my life,
Remembering my joys and triumphs,
My charity and my service to You.

God of forgiveness,
Here I declare my mistakes and misdeeds,
My regrets, omissions, and sins,
Asking for Your pardon and forgiveness,
Your understanding and salvation,
Your atonement and grace,
So I might return to You with a full heart.

Heal any harm I've caused
In my home or family,
In my work or in play,
Whether known to me or unknown,
Whether by design or by neglect,
So that after I'm gone
No one suffers from the consequences
Of my errors or misjudgments.
Free me of guilt or shame.
God of generations,
Hear my prayer.

M'kor chayim, Source of life,
May it be Your will that my passing be in peace.

שְׁמַע יִשְׂרָאֵל יי אלהינו יי אֶחָד!
Sh'ma Yisrael, Adonai Eloheinu, Adonai Echad!
Hear, O Israel! Adonai is our God! Adonai is One!

Tender End-of-Life Vidui

I did the best I could,
At least some of the time,
And more often as I got wiser.
My best got better,
And my shortfalls became more obvious.
This I ask of You, my God,
And of you, my friends and family,
And of any creatures or persons whom I've harmed:
Forgive me.
Release me from guilt.
Release me from my transgressions.
Release me from my mistakes.
In forgiving me,
You help me to forgive myself,
So I may pass from this world
With a greater measure of comfort and reassurance.
It is too late for me to do more,
And I ask with a heart of sincerity.

God of our mothers and fathers,
God of generations,
M'kor chayim,
Source of life,
May it be Your will that my passing be in peace.

שְׁמַע יִשְׂרָאֵל יי אלהינו יי אֶחָד!
Sh'ma Yisrael, Adonai Eloheinu, Adonai Echad!
Hear, O Israel! Adonai is our God! Adonai is One!

Travel to an Unexpected Family Emergency

Today,
God of old,
Is a day I never imagined
And never prepared to face.
I'm traveling
To be present as my _____
   [father/mother/sister/brother/child/wife/husband/partner]
Faces a medical emergency.
My fear is compounded by the stress of travel,
And I feel alone.

God of healing,
Bless _____ [name]
With healing of mind,
Healing of body,
And healing of spirit.
Ease his/her pain.
Remove her/his suffering.
Grant him/her courage and endurance
Throughout this challenge.
Bless her/his doctors with wisdom and skill
And his/her caregivers with compassion, focus,
   and dedication.
Grant her/him a full and speedy recovery.

Source and Shelter,
Give me the presence of mind
To be a source of wisdom and strength
In this hour of need.
Bless my family with ease and comfort.
Give us energy and endurance,
Hope, tranquility, and peace.

Blessed are You, God of mystery,
Source of health and healing.

Travel after an Unexpected Death

Today,
God of old,
Is a day I never imagined
And never prepared to face.

God of the bereaved,
Bless us as we come together
At this moment of desolation and despair.
Give me the presence of mind
To be a source of wisdom and strength
Among others who are mourning.
In this hour of need,
Bless our family with consolation and endurance,
Comfort and peace.

God of old,
Bless the soul of _____ [*full name*].
May his/her soul be bound up in the bond of life,
A living blessing in our midst.

Angel of Rest

Then came
The angel of death
With gentle words
And sacred tidings.
Quiet and rest.
Gentleness and peace.
Extending a hand and a smile.
A guide.
A companion.

In the end,
We are not alone
As we rise
Into the rhythm of light,
The expanse of glory,
The illumination of holiness,
To become one with the Infinite,
To become one with the pulse
Of the Divine.

Grief

In Sorrow

Ancient One,
Send light into this darkness
And hope into this despair.
Send music into this emptiness
And healing into this aching heart.

Air.
All I need is air.
A breath to give oxygen
To the anguish within.
A breath to give voice
To the howl in my heart.
A breath to set me free.

I am undone.
Crushed silent by sorrow.
Bereft by loneliness and loss.
Still yearning for healing.
Still yearning for love.
Still yearning for You.

Ancient One,
Send light into this darkness
And hope into this despair.
Send music into this emptiness
And healing into this aching heart.

Season of Sorrow

This is my season of sorrow.
A time when struggles recur and challenges arrive,
A time of endings and distress.
In this season I've known
Moments of pain,
Moments of sadness,
And moments of confusion.
I've seen
Times of loss and
Times of grief,
Moments that have stripped me of wisdom
And left me crushed and breathless,
Cold and in deepening shadow.

Holy One,
Help me recall my seasons of joy,
To recall with hope and praise
Your gifts and blessings.
Moments of laughter.
Moments of kindness.
Moments of peace.
Times of health. Times of clarity.
Moments that lifted my spirit
And comforted my heart.

In truth,
These joys and sorrows
Are gifts of holiness,
Gifts of mystery,
Gifts beyond my wisdom,
My knowledge,
My understanding.

Rock and Redeemer,
You are my comfort and my strength,
My light and my truth.

Sorrow at a Time of Joy

Sorrow comes,
Unbidden,
Amidst the routines of our days
And the joys of this life.

How much loss can one endure?
How much sorrow can one face?
Grief has arrived,
Casting a pall over the joys that remain.
Even as we celebrate,
We're overcome with distress.
Tragedy has struck.

God of comfort,
Help us through this difficult time.
Help us to be present for one another
And to find moments of calm and quiet,
Perhaps finding moments of joyous memory
    and laughter,
As we struggle together.

Upon Experiencing the Loss of a Pregnancy

Source and Shield,
You have made my body
To be a fountain of life,
A well of strength,
To take seed into the warmth of my womb,
To feed and hold,
To love and shelter,
To awaken new life.

Oh grief,
I am stripped bare,
The cradle of my body empty,
My heart bereft.

Oh sorrow,
My soul yearns, aches, weeps
For the one who will never rest in my arms.

Oh God,
Witness my distress,
My suffering and loss.
When will the days bring comfort and rest?
When will the nights bring solace and peace?
Hear my prayer.
God of our mothers,
God of generations,
Lead me on a healing path,
A path of wholeness and love.

Loss of a Pregnancy, for a Partner

God of old,
What can I say before You?
I am crushed,
Flattened by sadness,
Cut down by grief.
Yet my beloved needs
My courage and my tears,
My gentleness and my strength.
Our lives,
Once ripe with promise,
Feel vacant and hollow.
I have touched
A new loneliness and despair.

Rock of Ages,
Why have You raised our hopes only to take them away?
Why have You abandoned our prayers and our dreams?
What comfort remains?

Source and Shelter,
Teach me to honor, to balance, and to express
Both my pain and my fortitude,
My endurance and my sorrow,
In service to You,
In service to my beloved,
In service to myself.
Lead us out of this darkness,
Back to awe and wonder,
So we may know,
Once again,
Hope and joy,
Gratitude and peace.

After His/Her Infidelity

I thought that we were in love.
Was our past a lie?
Was I living a dream, a desire, a yearning?
After all we've been through together,
Was it false?
How long ago did your heart leave me?
How long ago did your hands and your eyes
Yearn for someone else?

Oh grief,
My soul is rent,
Torn apart by the one who promised
To help me find my way,
To help me journey through joy and sorrow,
To help me make myself whole.
You were once the warmth that held me.
You have become the blade that twists inside me.

God of compassion,
Grant me the strength to live a life of dignity and honor
In the face of this betrayal.
Help me to believe that there is light after this darkness.
Bless me with the time and space for healing.
Grant me the willingness to renew my trust in others
And the ability to trust myself
As I move into a new life.

God of mercy,
Be my hope when hope has left me.
Be my strength when my strength has crumbled.
Be my rock to anchor me.
Be my courage to persevere and to rebuild,
To choose, once again, a life of awe and wonder.

Hard Mournings

Mornings are the toughest,
That between time
When I'm not quite awake,
When my mind settles
Back to the familiarity and
The certainty of you.
Until I remember your passing.
Hard mornings,
Hard mournings,
Blend into evenings
Of solitude and sorrow.

Perhaps I'm wrong.
Evenings are the problem,
When the quiet surrounds me,
And the growing darkness
Shadows my heart,
Until blessed sleep
Descends from heaven.

Mornings are the toughest
New beginnings,
Each day an echo of loss.
Evenings are the roughest reminders
Of your absence.
Each night a hollow silence,
Emptiness in the space you once held.

One day
I will breathe again.
The Soul of the universe
Will turn my sorrow into dancing.
I will remove this sackcloth
And live again.

For Those Who Die Young

God of secrets,
God of my heart,
Source and Shelter,
Grant a perfect rest under Your tabernacle of peace
To _____ [*name*],
My _____ [*relationship*],
Whose life was cut off too soon,
Help us to remember his/her wisdom, talents, and skills,
The joy, laughter, and tears
And our moments together.
Let these memories continue to bless us
Even as we pray for her/him to find peace
In the world-to-come.
May his/her soul be bound up in the bond of life,
A living blessing in our midst.

Birthday, No More

This empty space in time,
In my heart,
Is yours, dear _____ [*relationship*].
It is the space for yearning,
The space of memory,
The day your light came into the world.
A day of sorrow for what was lost,
Birthdays that will never be.

This day touches
The depths of my grief and loss.
This day touches
A wound and makes it new.

God of generations,
Be with me [and my/our family]
As we remember what was
And what might have been.

I/we miss you.

After Shivah

The days have passed
And a quiet has settled on my home.
My grief still holds me.
My sorrow is present.
Yet You, God of seasons,
Ask me to look gently
Toward the future.
You, God of Creation,
Ask me to imagine a time
When the pain begins to fade,
A time when my hopes are renewed.
You, God of generations,
Ask me to honor life,
To cherish memory,
To love those who remain.

Source and Shelter,
Loving Guide of the bereaved,
Lead me on the path toward
Wholeness and healing,
Peace and comfort,
So that I become a well
Of compassion and strength.

God of old,
Your ways are secret,
Sacred and holy.
You are my Rock.
You are my Lamp.
Blessed are You,
God of all,
Who redeems the bereaved
With love.

Passing of a Beloved Pet

In sorrow and love
I/we remember _____ [*pet's name*],
Who provided [years of] companionship
And endless joy.
You were more than a pet to me/us,
Becoming a member of my/our family,
Providing consolation in times of loss,
Giving me/us laughter and delight
And a sense of well-being,
Rich with memories,
Rich in love.
The pain is deep.
The empty space
Too wide to comprehend.

[Forgive me/us, dear _____ [*pet's name*],
For my/our decision to remove you from
The suffering you endured.
We/I did it with deep sorrow,
Placing kindness for you above
My/our desire for more time together.]

God of the bereaved,
Grant me/us solace in the days ahead
And peace of mind as time passes.
Let my/our memories of the time/years together
With _____ [*pet's name*]
Be an endless source of wonder
In tribute to his/her memory.

Rest in peace.

Memorial Prayers

After an Accidental Death: A Yizkor Prayer

God of secrets,
Source and Shelter,
Grant a perfect rest under Your tabernacle of peace
To _____ [name],
My _____ [relationship],
Whose life was cut off without warning,
Cut off in a moment of inconceivable horror.
Even in this darkness,
Even in this grief and void that seem beyond repair,
Help us to remember his/her wisdom, talents, and skills,
Our times together,
Our joy, laughter, and tears.
Let the memories continue to bless us
Even as we pray for him/her to find peace
In the world-to-come.
May her/his soul be bound up in the bond of life,
A living blessing in our midst.

Memorial Prayer for a Child

My child,
Dear _____ [*first name*],
You are the love in my heart
And the tears in my eyes.
You are the longing in my chest,
A well of memories,
Joyous and crushing,
Holy and touched by sorrow.
My yearning for you will never cease.

God of all being,
Grant my/our son/daughter _____ [*full name*]
A perfect rest under Your tabernacle of peace.
Guide his/her soul back to Your holy realm,
For she/he left this world
Too young,
Too soon,
With dreams unanswered
And hopes unfulfilled.

Grant our family strength as we move forward,
A tribute to Your healing
In memory of our dear daughter/son.
May his/her soul be bound up in the bond of life,
An eternal blessing in our midst.

Yizkor after My Child's Suicide

Oh grief,
How deep was her/his pain,
That my child
Could take her/his own life?
God of old,
Grant a perfect rest under Your tabernacle of peace
To _____ [name],
My son/daughter,
Whose life was cut off by sorrow,
By hopelessness, depression, and despair.
Even in this darkness,
In this moment of inconceivable horror,
In this grief and void that seems beyond repair,
Help us to remember her/his wisdom, talents, and skills,
Our times together,
Our joy, laughter, and tears.
[Give me respite from this profound sense of guilt.]
In this hour of desolation,
Bring our family comfort and consolation
As we pray for her/him to find a new peace
In the world-to-come,
A peace she/he did not enjoy in this world.
May his/her soul be bound up in the bond of life,
A living blessing in our midst.

On Lighting a Yizkor or Yahrzeit Candle

A candle.
A flame.
A memory.

God of generations,
Grant a perfect rest under Your tabernacle of peace
To _____ [name],
My _____ [relationship],
Who has left this life and this world.
Let his/her soul find comfort.
Let her/his memory be a blessing.

This candle is for healing,
This flame is for hope,
Calling forth our joys and sorrows,
Calling forth our hours and our days.

God of our ancestors,
Bring me/us solace and consolation
In this moment of remembrance.
Let all who mourn find peace.

First Yahrzeit

Creator of all,
Source and Shelter,
Grant a perfect rest under Your tabernacle of peace
To _____ [name],
My _____ [relationship],
Who was taken from our midst one year ago.
The loss is still fresh and, still, healing begins.
Keep our memories vital and present
So that we may remember dear moments with love
And pass her/his legacy to the next generation.
May we live our lives as a tribute,
In service to our living God.
May these memories be sanctified with righteousness
    and charity.
May his/her soul be bound up in the bond of life,
A living blessing in our midst.

Second Yahrzeit

God of all,
Source and Shelter,
Grant a perfect rest under Your tabernacle of peace
To _____ [*name*],
My _____ [*relationship*],
On this second anniversary of his/her death.
My grief lingers.
Part of me is afraid to let it go,
Afraid that I will forget.
Give me the strength and wisdom to share the stories
    of his/her life
With wonder and joy,
A tribute to her/his days and years.
May these memories bless him/her in the world-to-come
And comfort those who remain.
Let me honor her/his memory
With acts of charity,
Deeds of loving-kindness,
And dedication to Your Holy Word.
May deeds sanctify his/her memory with righteousness
    and charity.
May her/his soul be bound up in the bond of life,
A living blessing in our midst.

Biographies

ALDEN SOLOVY is a liturgist, author, journalist and teacher. He's written more than 600 pieces of new liturgy, offering a fresh new Jewish voice, challenging the boundaries between poetry, meditation, personal growth and prayer. His writing was transformed by multiple tragedies, marked in 2009 by the sudden death of his wife from catastrophic brain injury. Solovy's teaching spans from Hebrew Union College-Jewish Institute of Religion in Jerusalem to Limmud, UK, and synagogues throughout the U.S. *The Jerusalem Post* called his writing "soulful, meticulously crafted." *Huffington Post Religion* said "...the prayers reflect age-old yearnings in modern-day situations." Solovy is a three-time winner of the Peter Lisagor Award for Exemplary Journalism. He made aliyah to Israel in 2012, where he hikes, writes, teaches, and learns. His work has appeared in these CCAR Press editions: *Mishkan R'Fuah: Where Healing Resides* (2012), *L'chol Z'man v'Eit: For Sacred Moments* (2015), *Mishkan HaNefesh: Machzor for the Days of Awe* (2015), and *Gates of Shabbat, Revised Edition* (2016). His latest works are posted weekly to www.tobendlight.com.

RABBI MENACHEM CREDITOR is spiritual leader of Congregation Netivot Shalom in Berkeley, CA, and the founder and chair of Rabbis Against Gun Violence. Named by *Newsweek* as one of the 50 most influential rabbis in America, he is a regular contributor to *The Huffington Post* and *The Times of Israel*. His books include *And Yet We Love: Poems*, *Not by Might*, *Primal Prayers*, *Peace in Our Cities*, *The Hope: American Jewish Voices in Support of Israel*, and *Siddur Tov LeHodot: A Transliterated Shabbat Prayerbook*. A musician whose song "Olam Chesed Yibaneh" has become an international Jewish anthem of hope, he also serves as a Trustee of American Jewish World Service and sits on the Social Justice Commission of the International Rabbinical Assembly. Find out more at menachemcreditor.org

Permissions

The following are reprinted with permission from *Jewish Prayers of Hope and Healing* (Kavanot Pres, 2013): My Child Leaves Home; The Path of Righteousness; For Creation; After Shiva; Your Name: Meditation at Dusk; Meditation for a Child's First Torah Reading; Yizkor for a Soldier; Praise the New Day; Season of Sorrow; This Ring; For Pregnancy; For Fertility Treatment (women); For Fertility Treatment (men); and Loss of a Pregnancy, for a Partner.

The following are reprinted with permission from *Haggadah Companion: Meditations and Readings* (Kavanot Press, 2014): Egypt Inside; The Season of Freedom; The Season of Counting; and For Spring.

CPSIA information can be obtained
at www.ICGtesting.com
Printed in the USA
BVHW04s0752240818
524955BV00006B/187/P